Know My Soul

Rudy Avila Gonzalez

BookLeaf Publishing

Presentation by *BookLeaf Publishing*

Web: www.bookleafpub.com

E-mail: info@bookleafpub.com

ISBN: 9789358368109

First edition 2024

DEDICATION

Thank You Lord, for allowing me to see this book to its completion.

To my mother, who has always spoken life unto me, even when I wasn't making the best decisions.

To my family who have always pushed me to do and be better.

To the U.S. Navy for allowing me to see the world through a broader lens.

To the women who have graced me with their presence.

To the reader, I hope you enjoy.

And to my Father.

ACKNOWLEDGEMENT

A moment of true introspection starts with a question leading into the depths of one's mind, heart, and soul. Knowing how to let go of the ego will give way to an endless sea of truth and vulnerability. So, the question to ponder is, do we know how to place our ego aside to foster a genuine space for truth and vulnerability? A genuine space to be able to ask, answer, and have a conversation about the hard questions that may be asked? How comfortable are we at looking into the mirror with eyes of hope and an open mind? … eyes of reverence, unlocking the unknown. Fear is only but a catalyst used to blind us to the treasures that are buried deep within. The events that occur which bring us to ask these questions are happening to us all … it's called life.

Most spend a grand amount of time trying to find or figure out their personal flow. But like any hidden treasure, a person must put forth the effort to discover what is buried. The unrelenting want and desire to uncover what is under the surface will benefit a person in multiple ways. A person learning how to be consistent, partnered with discipline is only one of the many keys through the doors of success. It's natural for a person to get fatigued, so partnership is necessary. Alexandre Dumas of the Three Musketeers famously said, "all for one, one for all," especially when it comes to accomplishing a goal.

The U. S. Navy taught me the importance of having 'all hands-on deck', the true meaning of teamwork. Within this construct, we come to realize that we are also helping someone else find the beautiful gems hidden within themselves. I want to make sure I say this clearly, change makes a person bitter while evolution makes a person better. Taking a good look at the people you have around you will give you a great perspective on which side of the fence you fall on. The beautiful part about life is if you don't like where you've fallen you can always get up and change the narrative.

FOREWORD

When I first met Rudy G. we were at a watering hole for Poets. After returning to Bridgeport, Connecticut from a three year stint where I was teaching overseas, I was eager to head to an Open Mic in Downtown at Poetz Realm to hear some poems and watch some performances. This fellowship with poets, artists, and musicians was something I longed for while I was away doing a bit of soul-searching myself.

When Rudy touched the stage, he carried with him a cadence that caught my attention. His poetry was clearly influenced by Hip-Hop and his delivery was silky smooth and poetical enough to put you right in the passenger seat with every line he strung together. My ears perked up as he flowed because although he rhymed and stacked syllables and words with ease, he was not chained down by rhyming. He would take the last two words of each line and make them fit so well together that even though they didn't rhyme they still seemed like a match made in Heaven.

As the show came to a close, I approached him to give him his props on a dope performance. After a few minutes of conversing and vibin' out, I soon learned that Rudy's regular voice was just as poetical and rhythmic as his performances are onstage. It became clear that Rudy's art is not just something that he wears when stepping on stage and takes off later, but rather a lifestyle and commitment to himself and our Creator.

I've been fortunate enough to have Rudy G. perform at several shows and events that I've curated and with every performance he brings the audience that much closer to catching a glimpse at the holistic artist he is and is still becoming.

It's clear that Rudy's words, songs, stories, and poetry will make their way around the world reminding readers that

Poetry is Pain,

Poetry is Progress,

Poetry is Passion,

Poetry is Powerful,

Poetry is Song, and

Poetry is Praise and Worship.

Whether you're a casual reader, a bookworm, a lover of lyrics or a poet yourself, *Know My Soul* is for you. It is a coming-of-age story, a testimony of stumbles and triumphs, and an ode to those seeking Self and Soul.

-     Balanc3

Five Stars Blue

As I live and breathe
I can be sure
Of one thing

… I'm different.

Since playin' tag
On the blacktop,
Scrapin' my knees;

I always knew
There was
Something different
About my DNA
When I'd bleed.

I never understood
What it was
Until my 5th grade teacher
Explained to me
That I can choose
Between bein'
African-American or
Latino.

I knew I was different
Since the first time
My Latin tongue
Made others
Double take
Because of my
Chocolate Brown
Complexion.

I was never confused
I just had a lot of questions.

That were never asked
Because the answer
Was before me
At the kitchen sink.

Washin' rice
While Celia Cruz
Played in the background.

Joy and laughter are twins.

Of this,
I'm completely convinced.

"La Negra Tiene Tumbao,"
My mother would sing
Ever so proud.

But we're not Cuban.

Dominicans
Gravitated
Toward us because
Most understood the history
Deep without our flesh.

And Puerto Ricans love us
'Cause there's somethin' to discover.

The first time
I ever had
A Colombian woman
Appreciate my history,

Was the same day
I stopped wonderin'
Why I was special.

God knew
What He did
When he made me.

Five stars.

Go deeper
Than the color red.

These five stars.

Far exceed
Any value
To consumerism.

Five stars,
Blue.

On top
Of white hues.

In between
The color blue.

When you see me
Black history
Coincides with
My Latin roots

… of independence.

Let me say it
One more time.

Just so
You can get it.

Five stars,
Blue.

On top of
White hues.
In between
The color blue.

When you see me
Black history
Coincides with
My Latin roots

… of independence.

Orange Hue

Orange Hue

Glad to say
Good Mornin';

To a precious
Sunrise?

The color is …

Orange Hue

Breathing in
The brisk fall air;

Takin' in
The changin' colors
Of the leaves,

Burgundy.

But don't forget the …

Orange Hue

Forgettin' that
You're made
In the image of
The MOST HIGH;

Are you practicin' meekness?

Or are you
Pickin' up
The pieces
Of your face?

Hello, stranger.

Where's your faith?

Is it
In a sunny day?

What if
The clouds
Come out
To play?

And the rain
Felt like bullets,

Pourin' into
A cup

Of pain.

Do you know
That it's all
Mental?

… push us all
To be better people.

So the
Cascadin' patterns
Of the rain
Drops

Fallin'
On my head,

Causin' pain
Stop.

I know
That the sun
Is shinin' somewhere.

And sometimes
I can
Forget to smile.

It's been

A while
Since someone's
Loved me.

But thank You, Lord
Because I'm not alone.

I often
Think about
The

Orange Hue
In your brown eyes.

Deep-rooted
To a beautiful foundation.

I see your soul.

Don't let
Those spirits
Take control of you.

You are powerful
Beyond belief.

Soul Speak I

Nine mils and AKs;

Revolvers,

Prepared
For a rainy day.

Thelma
Can sing
Her way
Out a storm.

And I've been here
Thankin' the Lord
That the sun's out.

Kissin'

Melanin
Queens;

Skin
On point,

Like a sundial.

I love
To see
The moon
Come out

When the sun's down.

We wake
The sun up,

And make music
Until we're all
Back to sleep.

Havin'
Conversations

Concernin'
The future

And what's to come.

The steps of a
Good man
Are ordered,

Hold fast
To these
Next words;
Know my heart.

O' Lord,

How could I
Flow casually

When I know
Who I are?

Roots
Deeper than
A mustard seed

Well taken care of.

Seein' faith
Take way

In the steps
That I tag

The world with.

When asked

What's a whirlwind
Compared to an ill bar.

The world, to me.

So I
Inhale,

And breathe
Hints of Heaven
When I speak.

Pro fit
How my words
Come alive
To a catchy
Rhythm.

Do I speak
In parables?

Apparently
My metaphoric
Quotes

Are comparable
To words
From Him.

So my songs
Are a gift.

I'm still here …
Livin',
Present.

Precious
Moments

I let go.

While my heartbreak heals.

And the mornin'
Brings in
A new perspective.

Make it Mine

Prince's
Paid the price
For this life
We yearn for

My heart's
On Betty White.

Pure,
Lust
For living
To the fullest.

Lord knows
I'm so ballsy.

Arrogance
Don't look good
On my skin.

O D Confident
With these lines
I give.

What's a gift
If you ain't 'gon
Use it,
Right?

And I'm blessed
To a modest form.

I've got the key
To open doors;

Now that's patience.

Here goes
The Little
Engine that Could,

Because he knew
That he would

And everything
Will be …

More than Great.

I see the world
Through a different lens.

The highest heights

I can't pretend,

I want more.

Battlin'
The man
I'm faced with

… every time
I look
In the mirror,

I see it too clear.

Champagne corks pop.

Though I don't drink

Here's a toast to more

…Opportunities
Come and go.

Peep your poker face,
Know when to fold.

But I'm playin' mine
Straight Ace's.

Honor Roll.

We make moves
Deemed honorable.

Momma been said,
"You outta control."

The risks we take
To get it goin'.

Lord knows …

My heart is Gold.

Charismatic

A different feelin'
You gain
When you know
You're gifted.

And my words
Are masterful;
At its simplest.

I ain't sayin'
I dumbed it down,
In no way.

I'm just playin'

A different game;
That's Wimbledon.

Simpletons might've
Missed it.

A back and forth

… interaction,
Of course.

A Hot Girl
Summer
Ain't got
Nothin' on
The cool
I bring

... I even scores.

A coup d'état,
If you will.

She'll call me,
"Boss,"
Or
"Chief stepper."

Not enough Indians

To move butter.

I do better.

Different decisions.

Wise business.

Adapt
And run with it,

Or fight change?

Hmm?

Either way
Evaluation's the game.

You can't
Complain
About rain
If you
Prayed for it.

And this tongue
Makes her cum.

A dollar will
Make her

Spin around

If you wait
For her.

And I've been
Moved on
To phase three.

Please,
Watch ya words
When you face me.

Happy Father's Day

As a young child,
I questioned if I were good enough.
My pillowcase was stained
From tears of anger and confusion.
I would act out
In hopes that you would notice me.
Nine years old when my mother and stepfather
made it to my parent-teacher conference.
I remember as if it happened five minutes ago;
My teacher said I was a bright student,
but she noticed something.
I could never seem to stop talking to the other
kids.
Which any person would attest to be normal for
a young boy.
But when my mother asked what was I talking
about that was so important;
I was reluctant to say I was asking the other
children about their father.
Questioning myself on why my father wasn't
there.

Sitting outside the door, waiting for my mother,
stepfather and I to be called;
I could see the other children sitting in the laps
of their patriarch.
I grew even more angry.
What did I do to make him leave?
What can I do to get him to come back?
If I ran away in search of him,
Would he welcome me with open arms?
What would he say to me?
What would I say to him?
Oh, I know what I would say.
I would ask how he felt on Father's Day;
Knowing his firstborn is being taught how to be
a man
by two young men and a woman who are
clueless
on how to do this.
Being raised by the streets isn't something to
brag about.
But I take pride in knowing that's part of who I
am.
An intelligent young man; I came to be, with the
help of my city.
No longer angry at the world;
On the contrary, I came to realize things
happened for a reason.
And I'm thankful that I'm more my mother's
child

than my father's son.
No knock to him.
I now smile from the burden that I carry
of breaking bad habits, cycles, and reliving the
same mistakes.

Something Wonderful

Keepin' genuine
Love around me,

It could be fickle.

Watch the energy
You harbor,

'Cause it's felt
From a mile away.

Wise choices
Wit' ya words,

'Cause they'll
Stick with whom

… ever you speak with.

Peep the sequence.

Always listen
To understand

Wait to
Rebuttal.

Constructive criticism;

Goes in hand
With give and take.

A better me
Is my epiphany
Of better days.

My ears
Stopped ringin',

They poppin' now.

If you know
You know,

I'm in a different
Atmosphere;

Lord, touched the ground.

In my humility
I walk in,

'Cause I'm far
From perfect.
Catch me
Dancin' in the rain,

Gettin' rid of pain.

Wash away my trauma;

Your smile
Is the Son's face.

Another way
To say

You shine, Beloved.

I call you King or Queen

Because we all
Come from
The Most High.

Although
At times
I feel it
On both side;

Lord,
Kill the flesh.

'Cause she loves
How I do it

With every stroke
Of my pen
(Pencil)
... Silk words
They poke nerves;

Uncomfortable?

Growth spurt.

You know

That you stand out?

Most Certainly.

Make room.

Those blessin's
They come through

To those
Who are diligent.

I feel
I'm the illest when

... I'm at my lowest.

Givin' thanks
To the All-Knowing
For every moment.

Inglorious or precious

Trust me,

They all
Work for somethin'.

Every lesson learned

Comes with
An abundant blessin'.

Diamonds don't break,

They're made
Under extreme tension.

Which is just
Another way
To say
We need
Pressure.

Keep bein' great.
Believe me,
They see your
Hard work.

Amazingly Blank

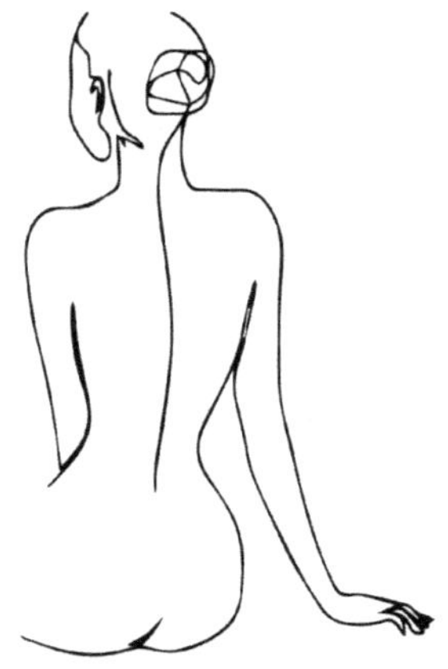

All the answers are in her eyes,
But there's nothing on her mind?

Straight,
Up and down;
But I found the cat with her tongue.

Charisma has never been so shy,
But those are not her name.

As bright as the flash from a fired gun;
But sometimes the pieces are a mismatch.

Passion is her drug of choice;

So when she raises her voice
I know she's on one.

Love never felt so warm and pink,
And our heartbeats match.

The words from her lips
Press on my chest with conviction.

I listen avidly,
With admiration as her thoughts spill upon me.
She tells me everything so easily,
Hopin' that her opening up to me
Would ease her discomfort.

Tell me everything; Tell me everything!

Okay

… I'll tell you everything.

The grass is yellow.
The sky is purple.
The clouds are gray.
The sun is yellow-orange.

The wind is the perfect puppeteer;
And every time it blows
I find myself holding onto You.

Imagination has me creating the wildest
Fantasies.

I sometimes struggle with tryin' to live a
Made-up reality.

Then again,
That is the purpose of a dream realized.
And she's beautiful

Man of Service

Love is patient.

Love is kind
And it's gentle.

We'll only boast
In the making,

Of something sweet.

And honey,

We flow
Like rivers of milk;

So Heavenly.

The only time
We'd ever lie
Is with each other

… and never to.

The only two
That comes to mind
Is Father and Son.

Understanding
That we are One
Spirit.

More than kindred.

You're made of I.

That depth

Is found
In your iris

… as brown
As chocolate gets.

And I get
The Eiffel.

Views of you
Do to those
Who don't have;

A wicked heart

Created in them,

Please don't covet.

I'm blessed

And it is her
I am cupping.

Cupcake.

Cuffing;

Coffee.

She is my cufflink.

Not an accessory;

She's the best,

Part of my side.

No excuses

She's down to ride

No matter
The tides
And waves ;

Our eyes
Are fixed
On the One

Above the clouds.

Lioness to my Lion
Is pride
In you I'm proud.

And I'm sure
God is too.

A Mother's Wisdom

Conversations
Wit' my moms,

And we talkin'
'bout life.

She asked me,
"What's next?"

I told her,
"I'm just try'na live right.

I'm try'na provide
For you
And all my brothers, alike."

She told me
She loves
The way
I keep my family
In mind.

But never forget,

"You gotta take care
Of yourself.

Remember I said

God is here for help."

I get it.

I'm in debt
For not payin' attention.

Lessons learned
In these streets
While I'm runnin' relentless.

I've seen
How life is precious,
While I'm chillin'
Where death is.

These flows
Could never be shallow,
These hoes
Is not where depth is.

Although a cloud
Is what I slept in.

And my head
Is inna crown,

Kept in.

I paint the perfect message.

Because I fell back
Doesn't mean I fell off,

I got the perfect method.

I'm here to stay

Like the gum
You stepped in.

I gotta solid flow,

That's ice

If you didn't know.

A few girls
Still love me,

But it's difficult.

My big brother
Still calls me from home.

He told me things crazy
Can't believe
He's there on his own.

Divide and conquer
Was the plan
From the jump.

I can't get comfortable
That's how you get stuck.

Keep your luck
I'm so blessed
In more ways than one.

Sink or swim?

I'ma jump
'Cause I know

I'ma fly.

Reachin' goals
Even though foes
Want me
To die.

Heart felt
Rhymes

Every time
I give you
These lines.

I love writin'
So much

I sit down
And I cry

... understanding
I'm unpacking my life.

Sunflower

 I do it
For the ones

That hit
The grave

… too early.

I do it
For the ones

That made
Mistakes

And never
Got away but

... Go away.

I do it
For the ones

That's in the yard

Right now;
Counting days,

'Til they out
The cage.

I do it
For the ones

That's in
Their lane.

Focused.

Workin'
Towards
A better day.

There's sunshine
After rain.

I do it
For the ones

Makin'
Ends
Meet
On the
Daily.

'Cause
They gotta
Stay fresh;

And babies
Gotta eat.

I do it
For the ones

Who didn't know
That life's a dream.

Funny thing

How I grow a conscience;
While I'm scrapin' guts?

Here's the parallel;

I do it
For the ones
That make it happen.

It's hard
Not
Feelin' like a King.

When you've gotta Queen,
Beside you.

Stimulatin'
Conversations
All around.

Energy
The color
Of

... Pink.

Not soft,
But floating.

Like sunset skies.

Or fresh-blown kisses.

Her thighs are

the Milky Way.

A different high
I describe

When I say,
"I'm kissin' stars
A like."
Dark skin
Match
Everythin'
That the stars
Would like.

Great energy.

Come alive
In the nighttime.

Just know
We blow
Fireworks
In the room
TOO.

Soul Speak II

Am I naïve
If I feel
The whole world
Can change?

Collective efforts
Can make it better

... More progressive.

Learnin' lessons
From way back ...

Then.

They do say

If you can't

Learn from your past

You won't
Live now.

My whole life
Wasn't rays of sunshine.
So I'll be damned
If I ain't
Dancin'
On a cloud.

Quite the high.

Let me break it down

I ain't
Even at my
Apex.

Lord knows
What's next
For me.

Let me
Not be
Deceived;

If I'm steppin'

To the rhythm
Of my heartbeat.

Uh oh.

Rememberable quotes.

From life
That I give.

The life
That I live?

Synonymous

To peace
On a boat.

How could I
Sleep;

If I'm
Wide awake,

Lucid dreaming?

Losing baggage?

No,

I'm lettin' it go.

Rights and wrongs.

Songs and poems.

Life
Is a rollercoaster ride,

And I keep my hands high.

Grabbin' the stars.

Handstand

That's me
Holdin' the moon.

My palms
Full of light.

Even on
The brightest day,
I'm still
Luminescent.

Outshinin' the sun?

Comparin' us both?

I'll be the latter.

I stay
Amongst great
Company.
The Holy Trio.

Fourth best

All Praise
To the One.

Humble brag
How I say it.

What you hearin'
Is amazing.

Thank You

GOD.

Lover Like

I'd love her like
I love me.

I'd love her like
I love You?

I'd love her like
I love us.

I'd love her like
Unconditional.

The good
The bad

The ups

And downs

The wins
And doubts.

There ain't
A doubt.

For every word
Out of my mouth

Is pure life.

VERSE I

And my light

I won't let
Dim down
For no one.

Big Bang

Is you and I.

When we collide.

Since I can't
Stroke you,

The way
I want to

Will you let
These words
Live in your mind?
A work of art.

Sunshine.

A work of art.

Moonlight.

I wanna be the

Tingle in ya spine.

Or those goosebumps
All over your skin.

When passion's
Made quick

Or forevermore.

HOOK

I'd love you like
I love me.

I'd love you like
I love us.
I can't love you like
I love God though

I'd love you like
Unconditional.

The good
The bad

The ups
And downs

The wins
And doubts.

There ain't
A doubt.

For every word

Out of my mouth

Is pure life.

VERSE II

For what's royalty
Without a Queen
By his side?

And my Kingship
Tells stories of victory.

I want to love you
Like God loves you.

Accepting your every flaw.

Understanding you are
Imperfect,

But perfect
In my eyes.

I want to love you
Like God loves you.

Knowing
Every hair on your head.

Down
To
Kissing
The heels of your feet.

I want to love you
Like God loves you.

So can you
Reveal
The darkest
Parts of your heart
To me

And unveil
Your most
Intimate thoughts?

So
Can I love you like
God loves you?

Now understand I'm flesh so

My love
Might be flawed.

But I'll try my best
To keep you in awe.

And in that line
Is humility.

Cause I know
I'm the bomb.
And I'll
Tic tic tic;

You off …

In the best way.

So what's patience
For timeless beings?

Kindred spirits
Are you and I.

It makes sense

Why I'm loving
Your vibe …

So can I love you
Like God loves you?

And He knows

HOOK

I'd love you like
I love me.

I'd love you like
I love us.

I can't love you like
I love God though

I'd love you like
Unconditional

The good
The bad

The ups
And downs

The wins
And doubts.

There ain't
A doubt.

For every word

Out of my mouth

Is pure life.

The Call

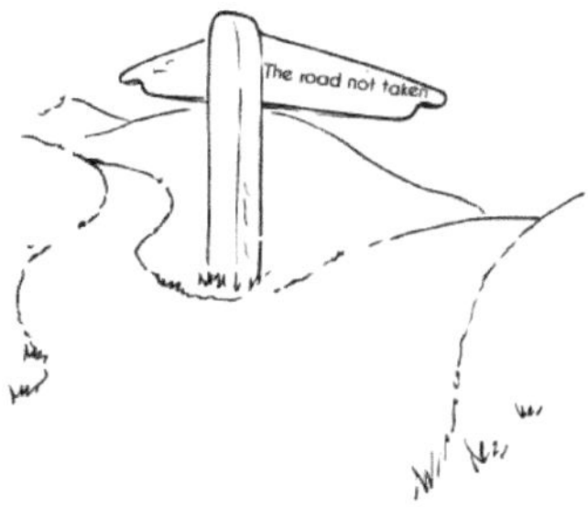

Some words
For my city,

Save the youth.

Holdin' fast
To a dream
While dodgin' bullets.

Fightin' back tears,

For the trauma
They feel.

Livin' life
To the full;

Without a peer,
A missin' smile.

Damn.

You may not
Want to hear it …

But you're here,
That's a Blessin',

Count 'em up.

This one's
For kids
In their room

Who feel stuck.

You're marvelous, love.

Don't give up.

And don't forget
You're a champion.

Yes.

You ARE beautiful.

Regardless
Of the nonsense
They may
Speak of.

Regardless
Of the nonsense
You might hear of.

Keep your chin up

Poke your chest out.

Keep the fire
In your eyes;

Smile big
For the picture

With no camera.

Talk about
The pain
You feel
Inside,

Or that damage will

… haunt you.

If you
Hold on to it.

Cleanse ya spirit.

Shed a tear
If you must.

And I ain't mad
If you feel like
Vengeance is the answer.

But vengeance
Is the Lord's.

Take a different course.

Life is out here
Not behind
Them bars.

Not everybody's
Livin'
What they
Talk about.

Smoke and mirrors.

I don't
Need a mirror,

I know
What Shekhinah looks like

With my eyes closed,
Too vivid.

Who are we
To destroy

A livin'
Masterpiece?

Art in motion.

Pick a part
Your emotions.

Don't let them
Control you.

Chosen

I've got
Joy in my heart,

I've been
Playin' my part.

I've been lettin'
Things go,

That I can't control.

Makin' peace
With my demons;

God
Sees 'em
Creepin'.

Plus
I've got
Power and authority
Within my hands.

At my fingertips …

Is every blessin'
That I could want.

Askin' God
To please
Search my heart.

Open the vault,

I wanna know
My flaws;

Apologizin'
For my
Each and every fault.

How could I
Feel so big,

But yet I'm
So small.

A humblin' presence
Only few subscribe to.

And I don't try to

... I just do.

Peace and Love
Whenever I sway,

Catch the vibe.

And He's still alive.

As long as
I've got breath
Within my lungs;

I'll smile wide,

Fightin' through trauma.

Subdued by grace
I've gotta
Thank my momma.

Inner conflict
Arises when

You do things
Contrary to your beliefs.

A power struggle;

Check what I mean

Things can
Only go
One Way?

I know
Who made me.

Breakin' the mold
Is known to be
Necessary
In fostering growth.

Who would've
Thought

A new page

Would uncover
All that hidden pain.

Kiss those paper cuts …

Mend them up …

Love your wounds …

Let them
View you
In sane;

Livin' out ya mind.

A monsoon
Will arise,

Tap dancin'
On water.

Seconds,
Minutes,
Hours,
Days;

Can feel like
A lifetime,

But do you know
You're in
His hands?

A smile

Can make
Gray clouds
Have to
Run and hide.

And pride
Shakes the hand
Of ego,

As far as we know.

Jubilant
When
Reaching a goal

Exuding success.

Eureka moment,

Exposin' Your genius
When explodin'.

And I don't want it all.

I just want
What's for me,
Lord.

Not the world.

'Cause it's too wrong.

Yet, my two stone
Made plenty
Of tombstones.

And if you
Haven't sinned

Then your skin
Might be
Two-toned.

Deep.

Recognizin'
My callin',
And yes,
I answered like,

"Really is it me?"

Wakin' up
In disbelief like …

HE chose me?

Sometimes

I wake up,
And I forget
To choose GOD.

Recognizin'
My flaws.

Still,
He chose me.

Then
When I remember

That HE loves me
Through it all,

I go
Run into
HIS arms.

Seers

HOOK

Close my eyes
And see
That I'm somebody.

Thank You, Lord,
For what You've done
For me.

I wake up
Thankful
For a new day
Always.

Waste no time
It ain't
'Gon wait on me.

I've got to do somethin'.

Baby keeps cryin'.

I've got to do somethin'.

Bills pilin' up.

I've got to do somethin'.

My girl's stressed out.

They waitin' on me.

VERSE II

I wish
I could
See myself

Through the eyes
Of another being.

Jumpin' over
Obstacles,

I won't
Call them
Hurdles.

Although
The pain
That is felt;

Is necessary
In buildin' character.

Don't lose hope.

The jokes on them.

Blinded by
Greatness.

As I …

Maneuver
Through the mysteries
On God's land.

Steady prayin'
That He don't
Let me go.

Life gets difficult.

And I'll be damned
If I'ma just roll

With the punches,

Dawg, I'm swingin' back.

Steady paces
As I water patience.

The force within me;

It's only right
I acknowledge You, Lord.

You accepted
My flaws
And all,

Your words
Beyond me;

Gorgeous.

Most wrestle
With the notions of truth.

I'm deep in it.

Like a baby
Nestled
On his
Mother's
Chest

For a meal.

And I've been steady,
Focused
On a way
To make
A Mil.

Yum.
(Million)
Yea,
These babies
Gotta eat.

And them bills
Ain't gone
Take care of
Themselves.

Dig what I mean?

So I keep my eyes
Focused
On the
Goal.

Soul Speak III

Self-preservation.

Create your
Boundaries,

Don't break 'em.

Understand
The law of respect
Works two ways.

Self-respect

Shows character;

It speaks volumes

To deaf ears.

I said something

… without moving my lips.

It takes action,

So put into practice.
Self-preservation.

Unlearn
Bad habits
and behaviors;

A different degree.

Embrace the change

That comes with
Overcoming
Affliction.

What's growth
Without pain?

Like what's May
Without rainstorms?

A tree
Is only
Dormant
In the winter.

And roots
sprout when they're
Sprinkled with love.

Practicin'
Gratitude
Is how to stay joyful.

Authentically
Givin' thanks
To the Most High

For splittin'
My hairs
To a new day.

I found me
A new way

To hold on
To Husain's
Right shoe.

I'm not crazy.

I'm out of my mind.

Since Out of
The Box.

Abnormal is
What normal isn't.

A masterpiece
With peace
On my tongue.

I'm at Pisces
With the flow.

I tune
A different
Pattern
When I write
My notes.

School's in session.

Self-preservation.

Keep your morals
And standards.

Don't break 'em.

Move humble.

Yet I walk
My fly
Perspective.

Overstandin'
My worth.

I'd love me, too.

Marvelous
In more ways
Than one.

Spectacular.

I know
I'm quite
The spectacle.

And so are you.

God's Child.

The sunbeam
Compliments

Our complexion.

Simply stated.

He created us.

More than amazin'.

With grace like a Dove.
Some
Cunning like
The tongue of
Anacondas
Cunnilingus.

I'ma spit it
Till they
Get it.

Self-preservation.

It's more
Than makin'
A statement;

It's how we breathe.

It's deep
Within us,

A different breed.

Remised to say
A pedigree
That goes beyond
The atmospheric pressure.

Divinity
Is what I speak of.

Your words
Are powerful

Spread love
When you
Express
Your thoughts
And feelings.

Regardless
Of what's
You're feeling.

Even
Your crumby days
Can satisfy
Those with

Exquisite taste.

Serve up
The whole pie.

I know
They will
Enjoy
The entire
Plate.

And then some.

Holy Water
To wash it down;

Vino.

Truly blessed.

We know.

Even when
Frustrated,

I'm at my best.

Wringin' out
Towelettes

Full of fears.

Collector of tears

Would never
Let me down.

Every word
I speak
Is confident,
BLOOD.

Driving out
Doubt,
BLOOD.

I'm here
To shake
The world up
BLOOD.

Thank You, Lord
For shedding Your
BLOOD.

So precious.

Self-preservation
Means nothing

When understanding
True dominion.

Fear of God
Is the beginning
Of all wisdom.

Bar-none.
I don't have
A bottle
In hand

But I'm walkin'
With the Spirit.

So gifted.

I've gotta
Remind myself
To live
In the moment.

I don't miss it.

Letting go of tradition

Is understanding
A blessing

Is given
To bless others.

So
I ask you,
My beautiful people

What's self-preservation?

Pieces

HOOK

I know You smile.
When I smile.

I feel You smile
When I smile.

I love your smile.

Spread the Love.

Let's rejoice together.

VERSE II

I need peace is …

Understandin'
My vibe is

So
Connected to
Immaculate Conception.

You heard …
The energy
That's carried through
My each and every verb?

Each and every letter is

Pistol Pete
On the reload.

This for my people …

Who understand
That this candy cane city
Ain't so sweet.

City of
Saints and fiends,

Righteously
Walkin' in between 'em.

Bob and weavin',

Fighting demons,

As I walk in purpose.

Look into
The eyes of a man,
Can you tell
He's hurtin'?

Fist bump
Conserve energy,

Then some.

Shake a hand
To feel Divinity,
Strike us.

Who am I
To think
I'm better than?

Lesser?

Nope.

Every word

I speak
I pray
That it
Gives you
Hope.

A street corner
Is colder
Than dollar bills
Foldin'.

Conversations
Through a penny
Bouta add up
Nice.

Thank You, Lord
You took account
Of my every
Flaw.

Shouting
Shimmy shimmy ya;
Throwin' hands
With stars.

Bit the moon
Then sat back
Just to watch her grin.

Givin' up
Control
Is something
That could
Bend the mind.

I lift my hands
To let her know
Of who I am.

Watched her dance
On my pinky;

More melodic
Than birds' notes.

I always
Stick my landin',

Don't compare that
To cliff notes.

I'm something special.

I Still Love You

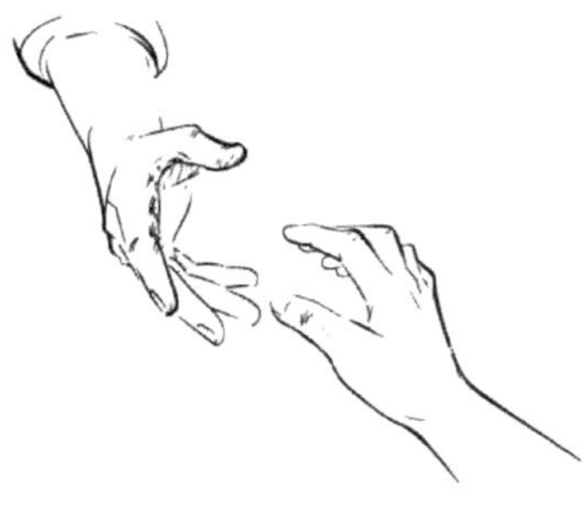

Focusing
All of my
Energy on

... Self-improvement.

The more
You know,

The more
You expose;

Lord, keep me.

The road
Less traveled on

Ain't for the weak or

Faint of heart.

Elohim built me strong and

My foundation
is A-UNO.
Heart big
'Cause my God
Created it large.

And you and I are
The difference between
Pluto and Mars

... Out of this world.

Ideas
Spew through
My vocal cords;

Holding on
Will only hurt you.

I'm understanding
Patience is a virtue.

Hurt people hurt;

Thank You, Lord,
'Cause I know my worth

Is pure healin'.

The more
I dive in,
More is revealed.

Truly revered.

What is fear of man,

If we all
bleed the same?

if we all breathe
the same
Air

… Jordan
how I'm floatin'.

My aura
is more

Divine
Than this flesh.

Defined by my best,

Which is now.

And not by my past

... Errors.
I'm in a new era,
No cappin'.

Salute
When you
See me,
Skipper's
On board.

I'm doing
Too much
To ever
Be bored.

I need some R&R

Choose an island.

BOOGIE DOWN

Where I get

My style from.

Momma love
Is where
I get my hustle.

Poppa bear
Was kicked out
For being a charmer.

Go figure,
Then there's me.

Young King,
Just know
I still love you.

Dawn of my days
Giving You praise.

Lord,
Keep me.

Eloquent
With words,

'Cause You
Gifted me with them.

Letting people go
Because
I ain't
Supposed to be
With them.

Birds of a feather?

I'm flying alone

… soarin' eagle.

Strip me of my ego,
If I still have any.

Prayers for my enemies,

I hope you succeed.

And my feet,
Will forever be
Victorious.

Givin' You …

The glory in
All of my ways.

The Holiest Spirit

Directin' my paths.

So yes, you can have
The last laugh;

I keep a smile on my face,
'Cause I've got
Joy like a river.
Enjoyin' my DNA (dinner.)

That's a metaphor,

No need for explainin'.

A different game
That we're playin'.

And the scoreboard
Is tithed to my favor.

Tryin' my best
To live
Like my Savior.

But there're so many flavors.

Guard your heart
Young Kings.

Guard your heart.

Bible taught you
That these women smart.

Gotta play ya part.

'Cause if not
They'll walk
All on ya.

The spine
Isn't a tightrope.

I look
To the Maestro

My feet
On the ground,
Firm.

My words
Givin' life, too.

Who knows
What I might do.

Serendipity can be a miracle
If you pay attention to it.

And there ain't
Nothin' to it
But to get it done.

Holy One,
Yes,
I Still Love You